# This Book Belong To :

..................................................................

..................................................................

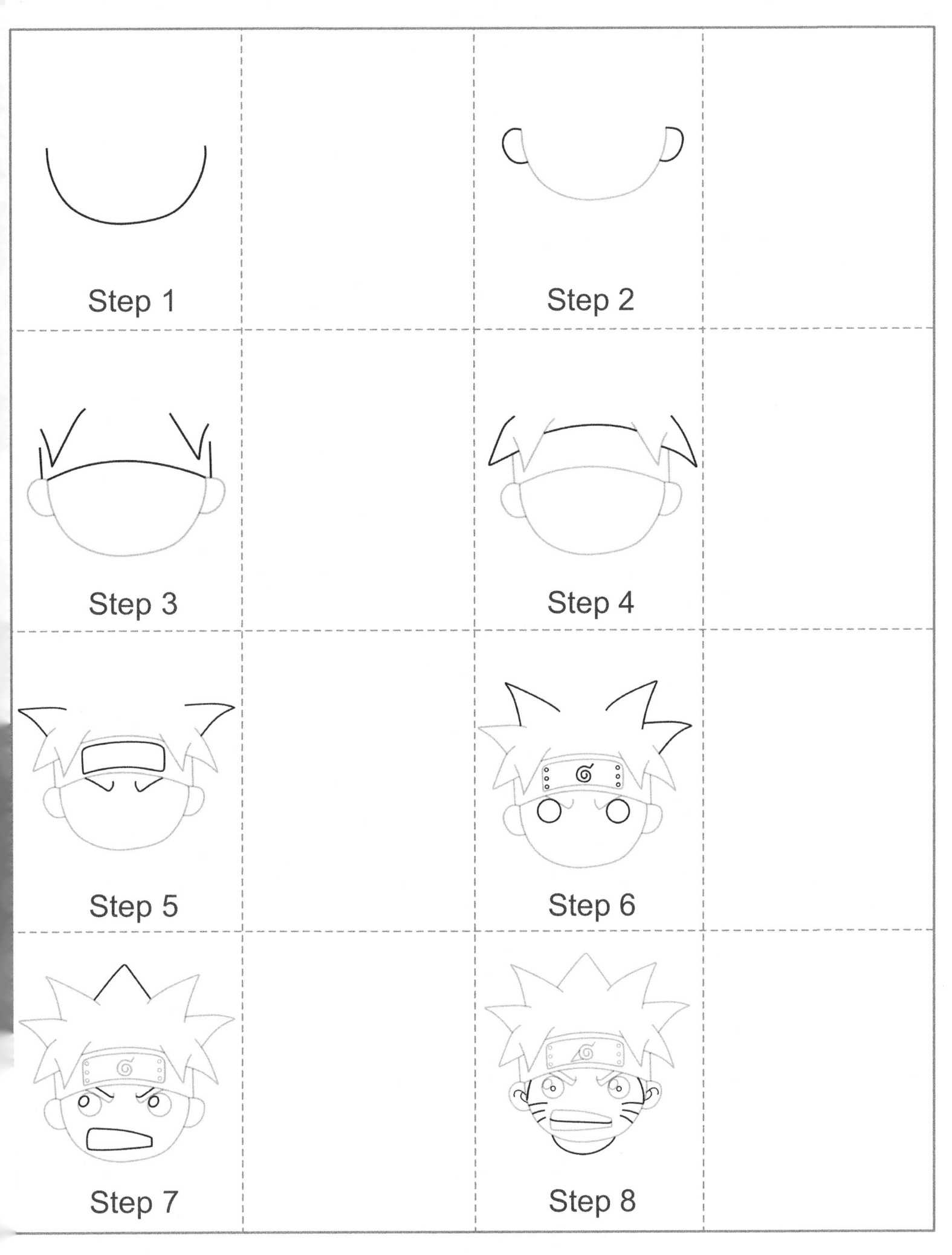

Step 9

Step 10

Step 11

Step 12

Step 13

Step 14

# Trace It!

## Complete the Drawings!

# Your turn !

## Friends ratings

Name : ........................ ⎯⎯ / 10    ☆ ☆ ☆ ☆ ☆    Name : ........................ ⎯⎯ / 10

Name : ........................ ⎯⎯ / 10                            Name : ........................ ⎯⎯ / 10

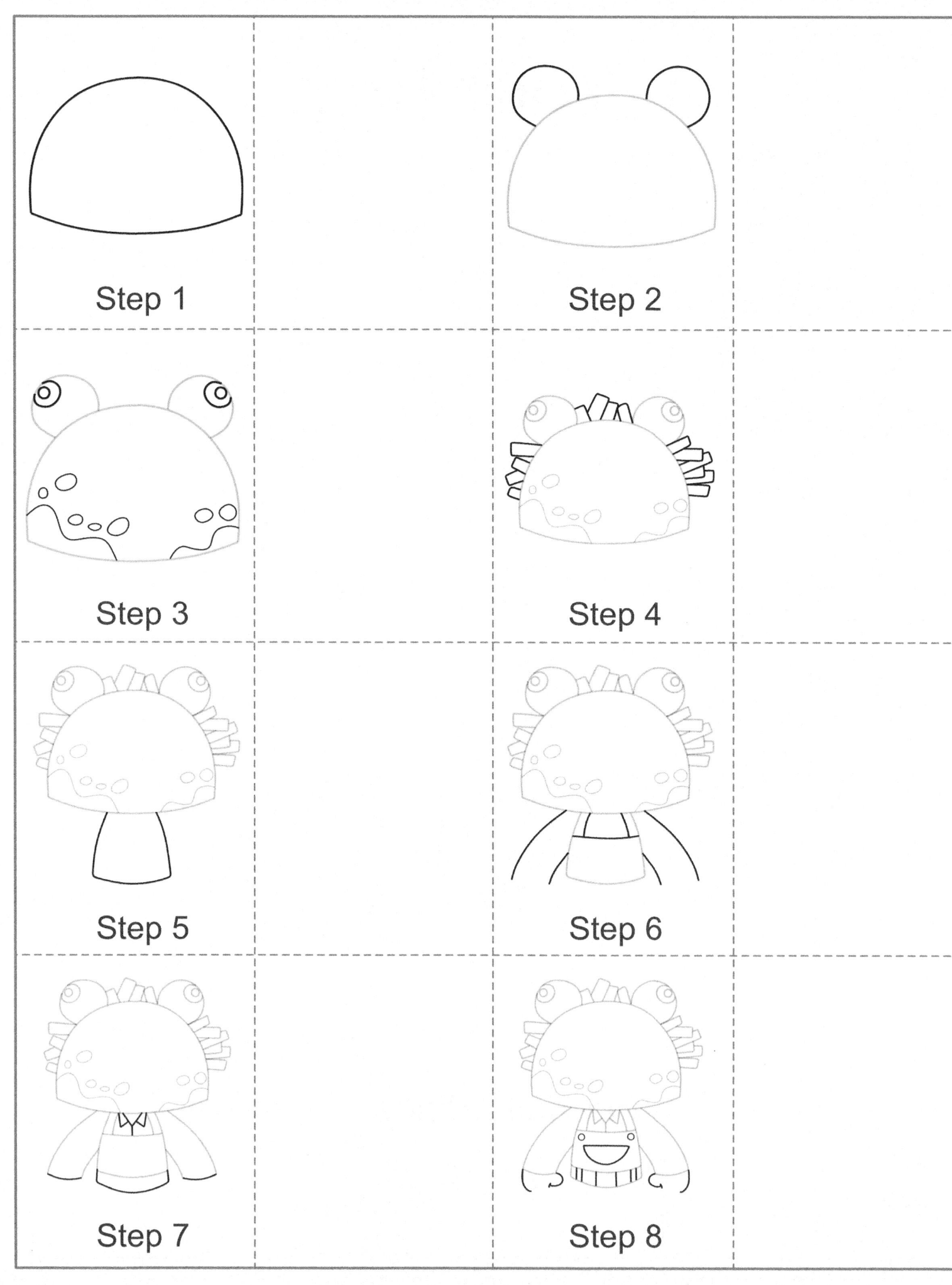

Step 9

Step 10

Step 11

Step 12

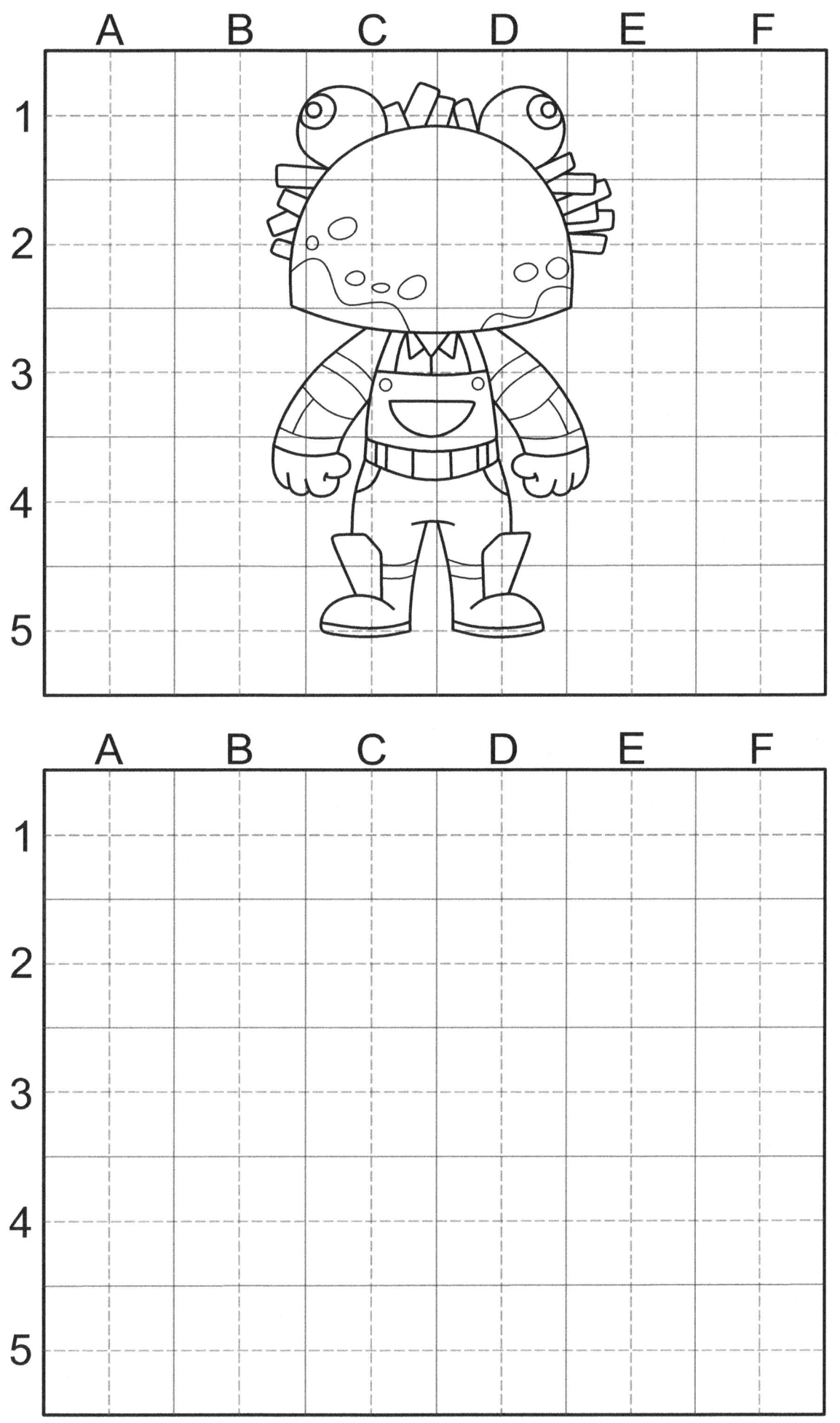

# Trace It!

## Complete the Drawings!

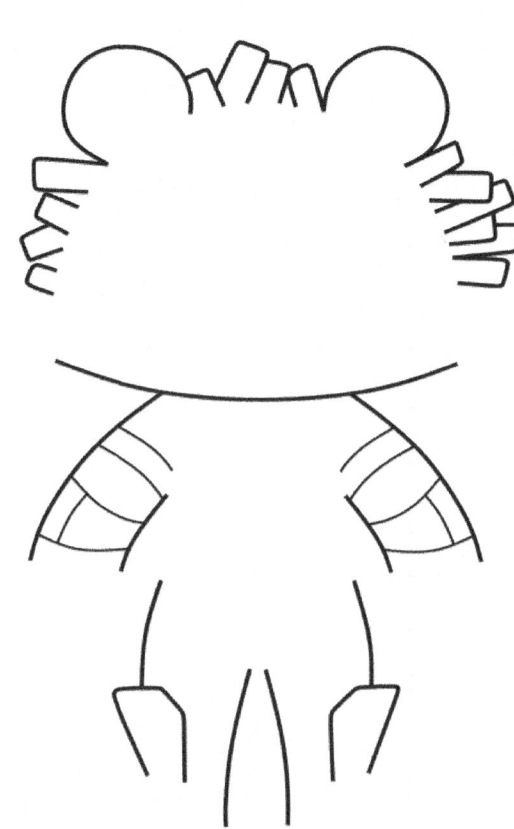

# Your turn !

---

**Friends ratings**

Name : ........................ $\overline{10}$   ☆☆☆☆☆   Name : ........................ $\overline{10}$

Name : ........................ $\overline{10}$                         Name : ........................ $\overline{10}$

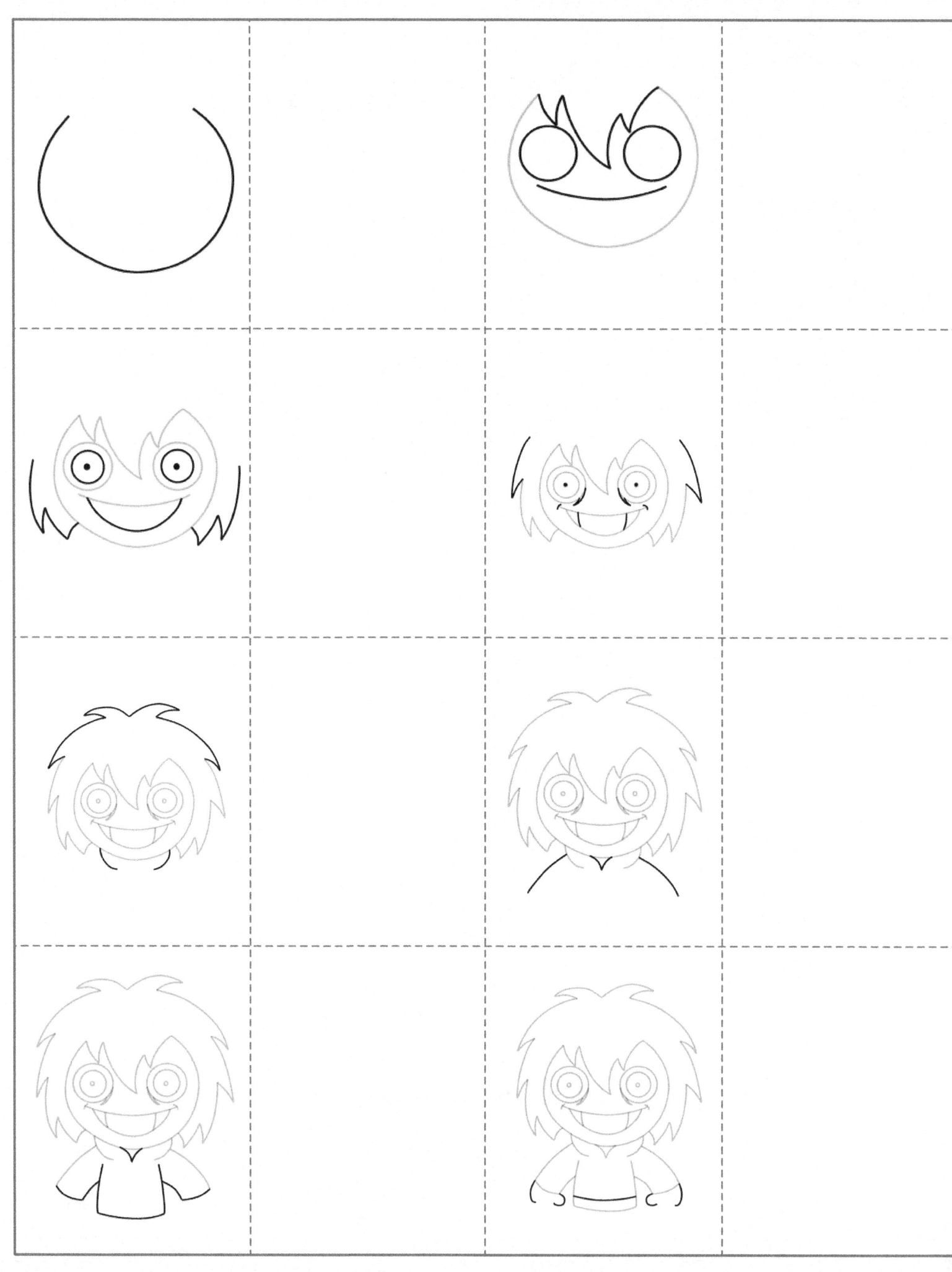

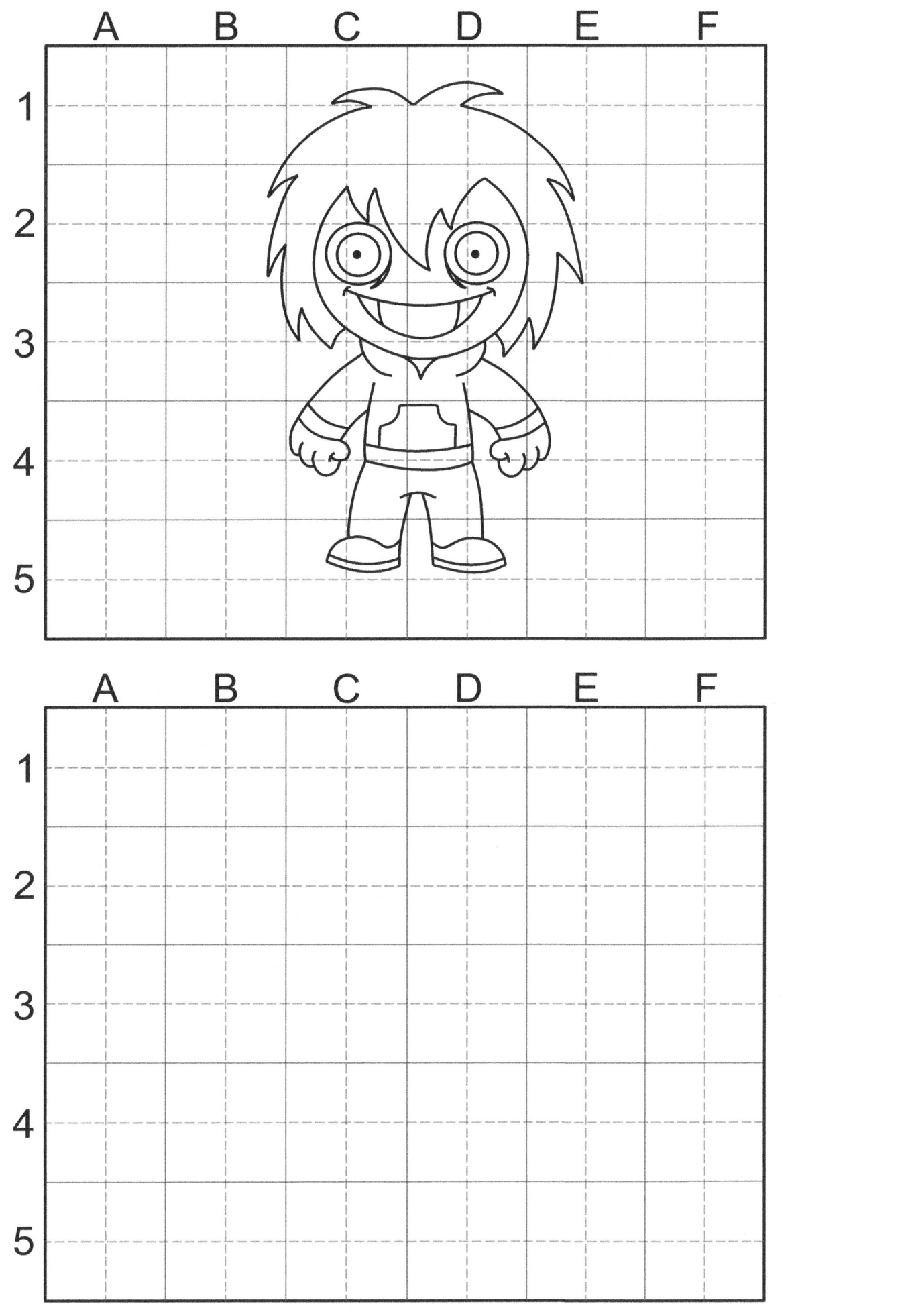

# Your turn !

---

**Friends ratings**

Name : _____ $\overline{10}$   ☆☆☆☆☆   Name : _____ $\overline{10}$

Name : _____ $\overline{10}$                Name : _____ $\overline{10}$

# Your turn !

---

**Friends ratings**

Name : ............... $\frac{}{10}$   ☆☆☆☆☆   Name : ............... $\frac{}{10}$

Name : ............... $\frac{}{10}$   Name : ............... $\frac{}{10}$

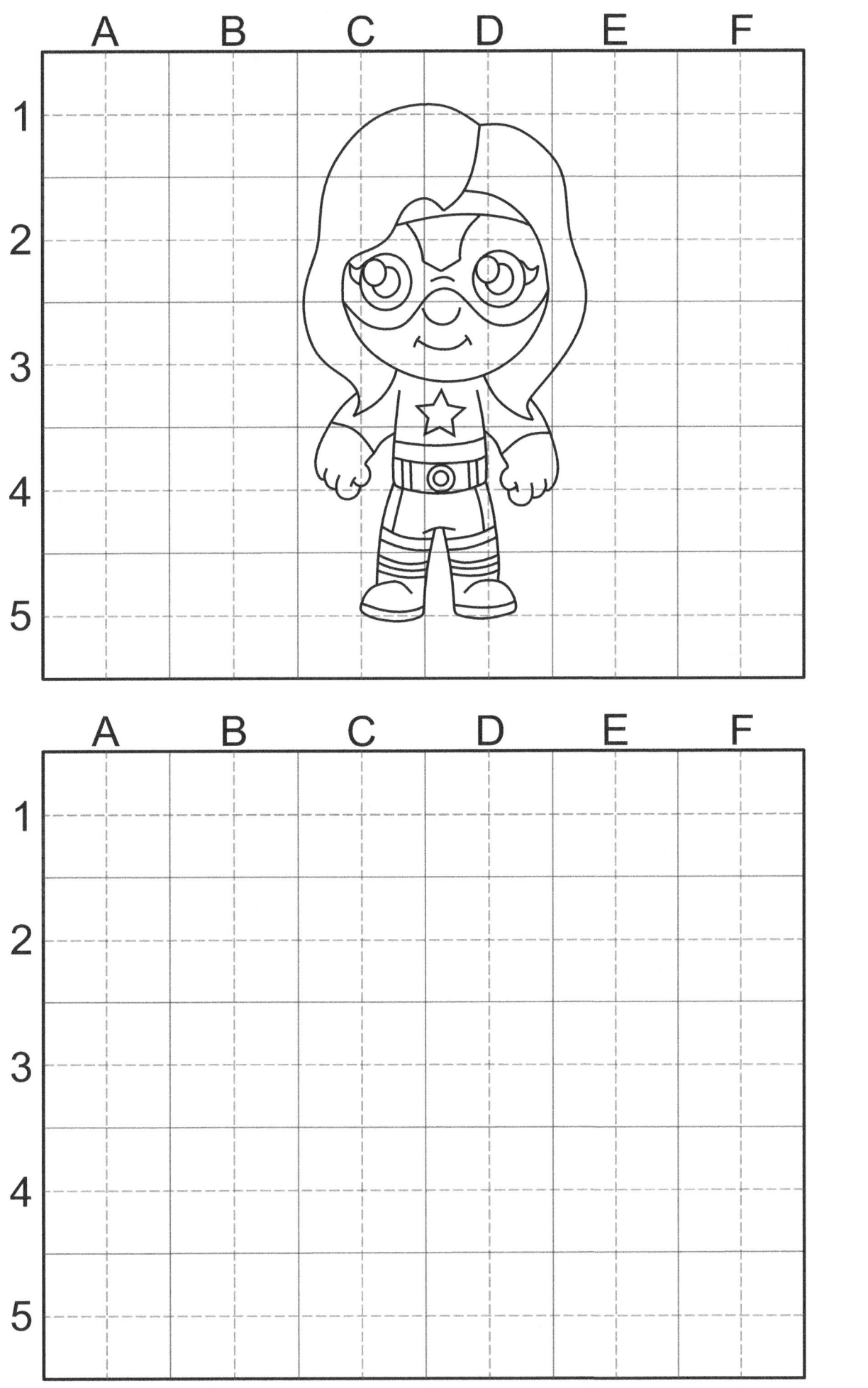

# Your turn !

## Friends ratings

Name : .................... $\overline{10}$ ☆☆☆☆☆ Name : .................... $\overline{10}$

Name : .................... $\overline{10}$ Name : .................... $\overline{10}$

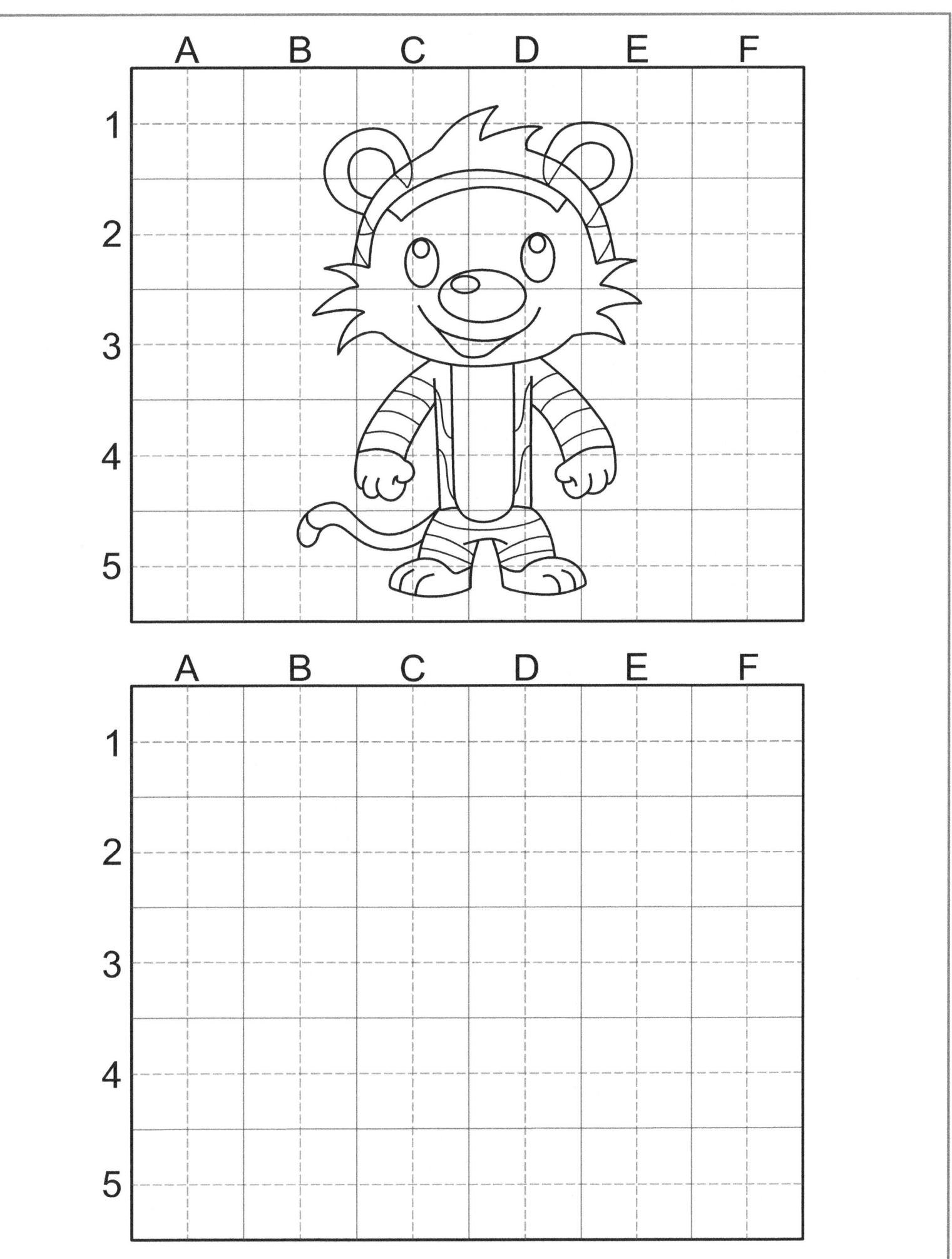

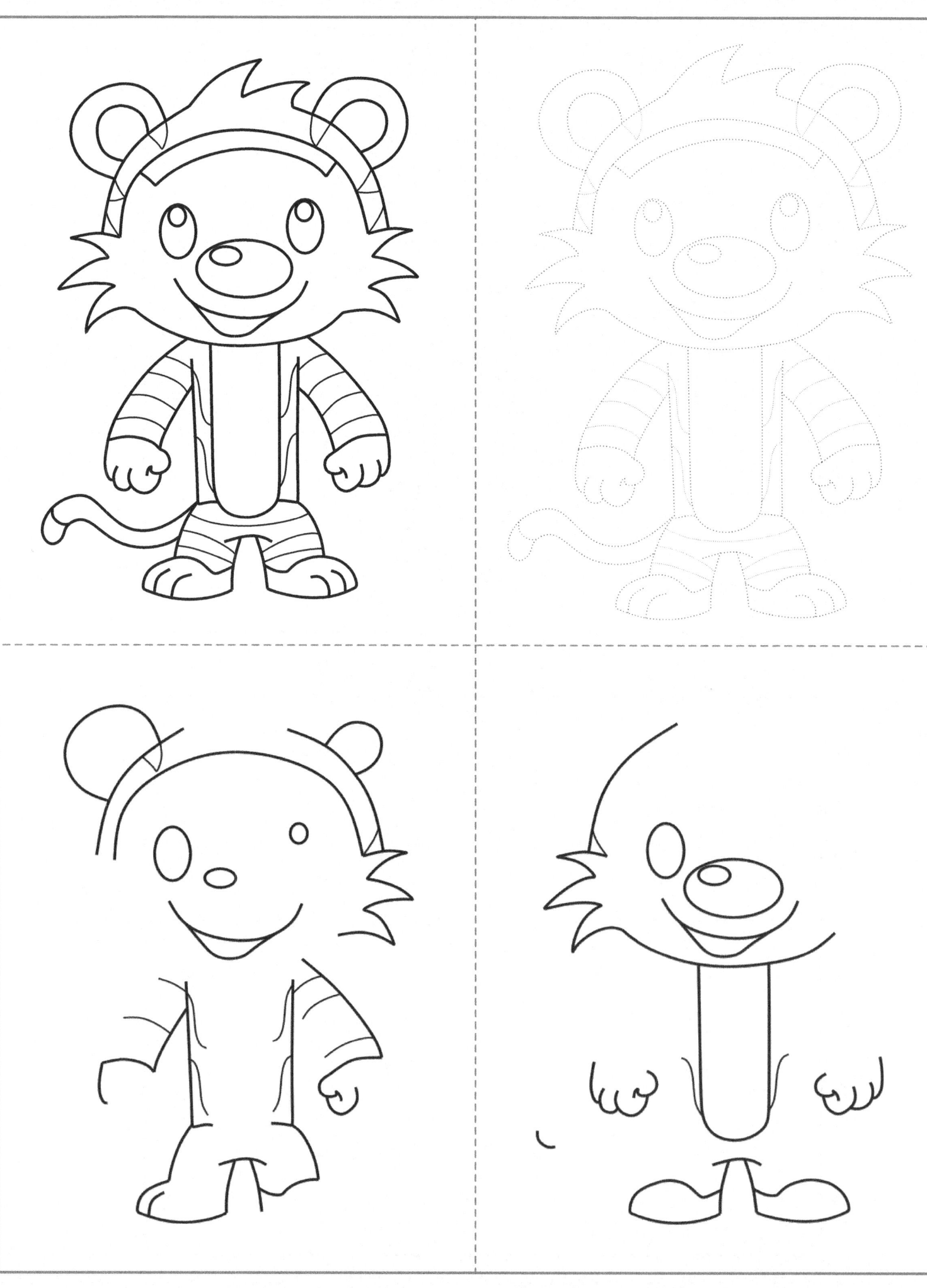

# Your turn !

## Friends ratings

Name : .................... $\overline{10}$

Name : .................... $\overline{10}$

☆ ☆ ☆ ☆ ☆

Name : .................... $\overline{10}$

Name : .................... $\overline{10}$

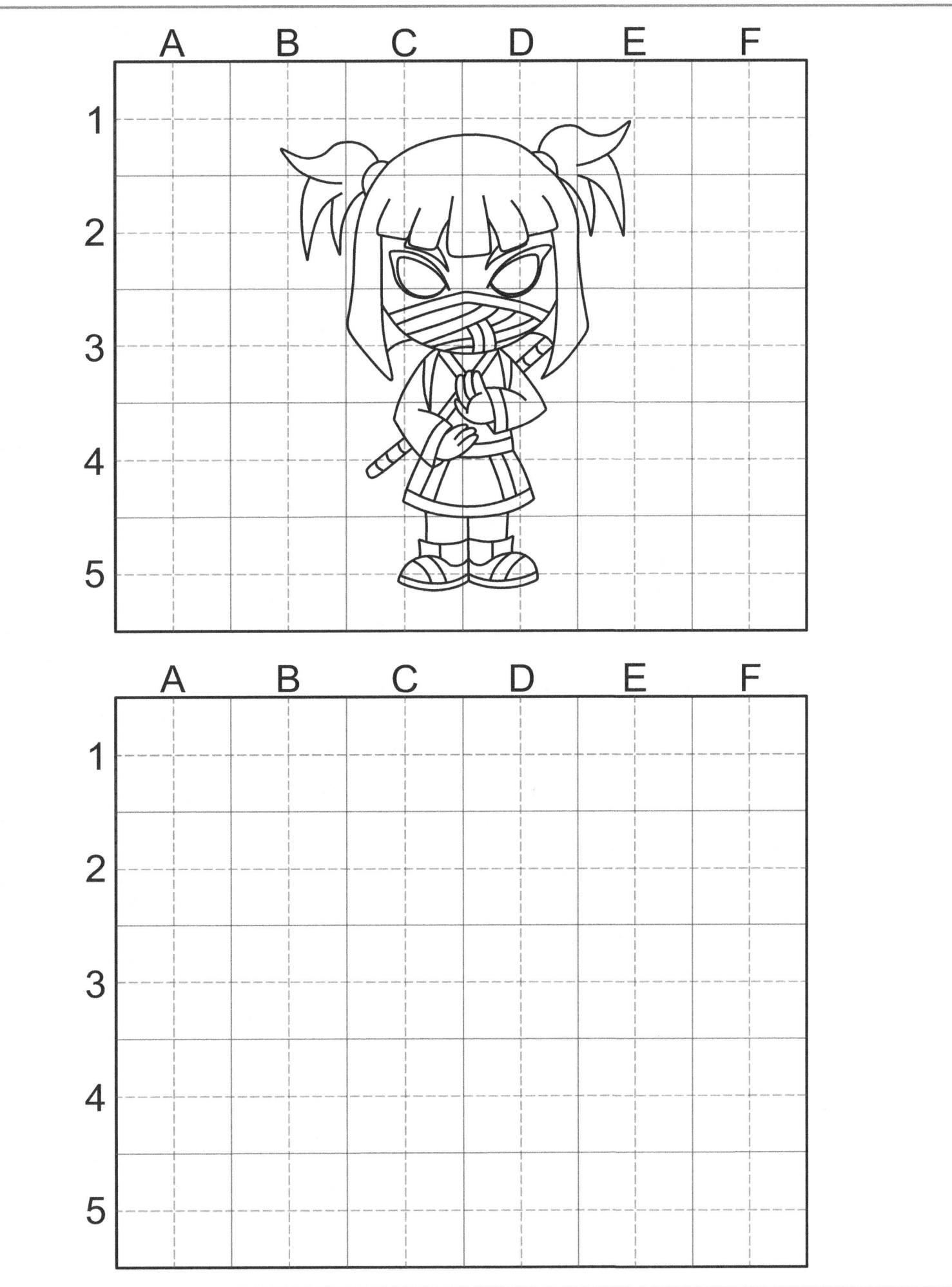

# Your turn !

## Friends ratings

Name : ........... $\overline{10}$  ☆☆☆☆☆  Name : ........... $\overline{10}$

Name : ........... $\overline{10}$     Name : ........... $\overline{10}$

# Your turn !

## Friends ratings

Name : ........ /10    ☆ ☆ ☆ ☆ ☆    Name : ........ /10

Name : ........ /10                    Name : ........ /10

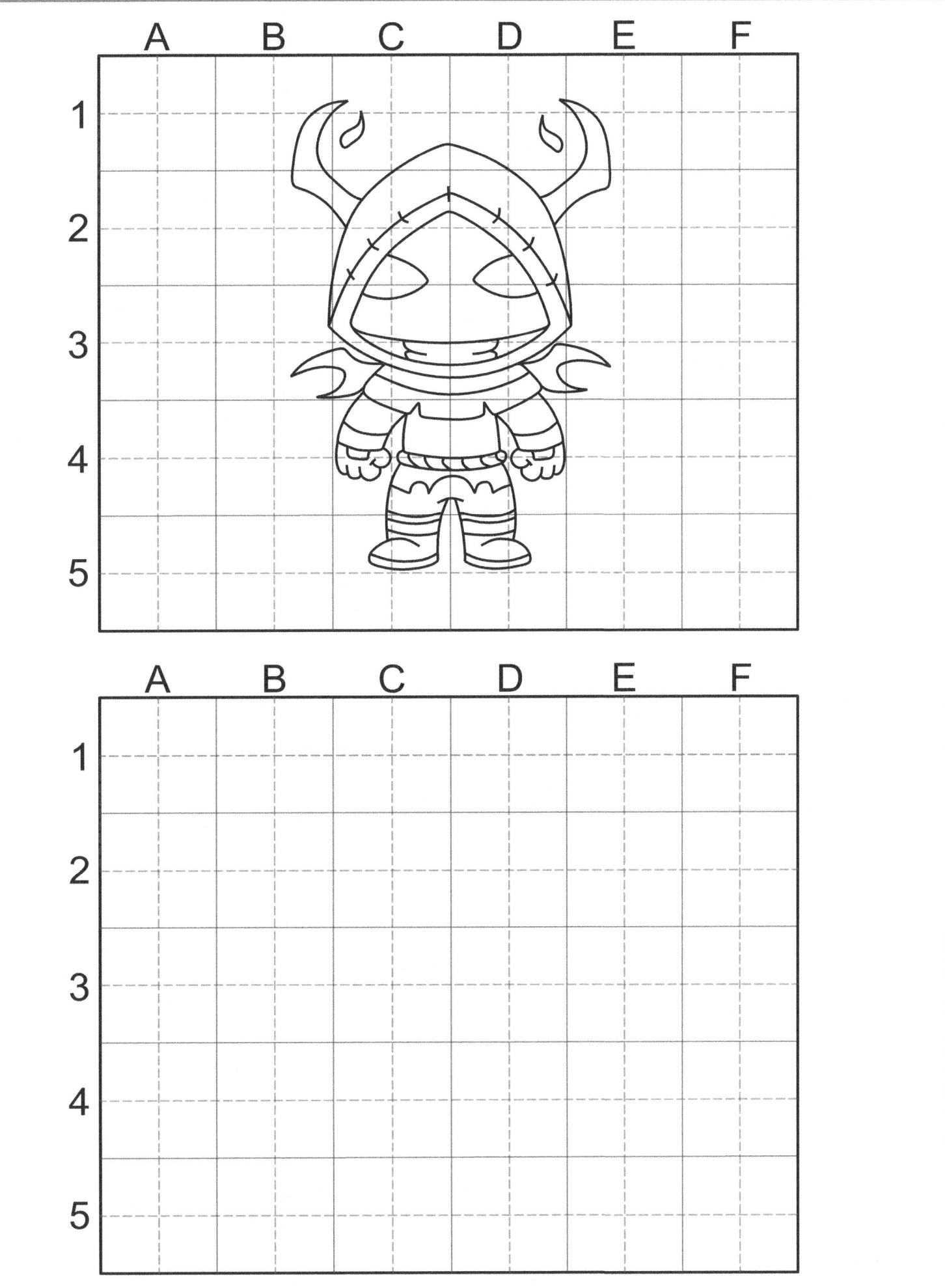

# Your turn !

―― **Friends ratings** ――

Name : .................... $\frac{}{10}$  ☆☆☆☆☆   Name : .................... $\frac{}{10}$

Name : .................... $\frac{}{10}$          Name : .................... $\frac{}{10}$

# Your turn !

## Friends ratings

Name : ........................ ⬜/10   ☆ ☆ ☆ ☆ ☆   Name : ........................ ⬜/10

Name : ........................ ⬜/10   Name : ........................ ⬜/10

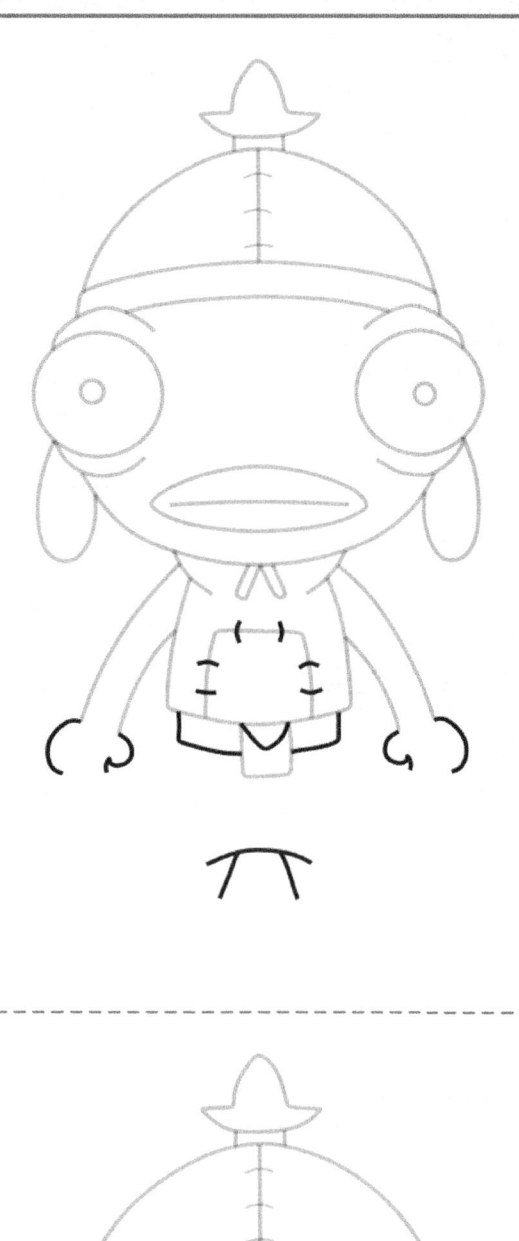

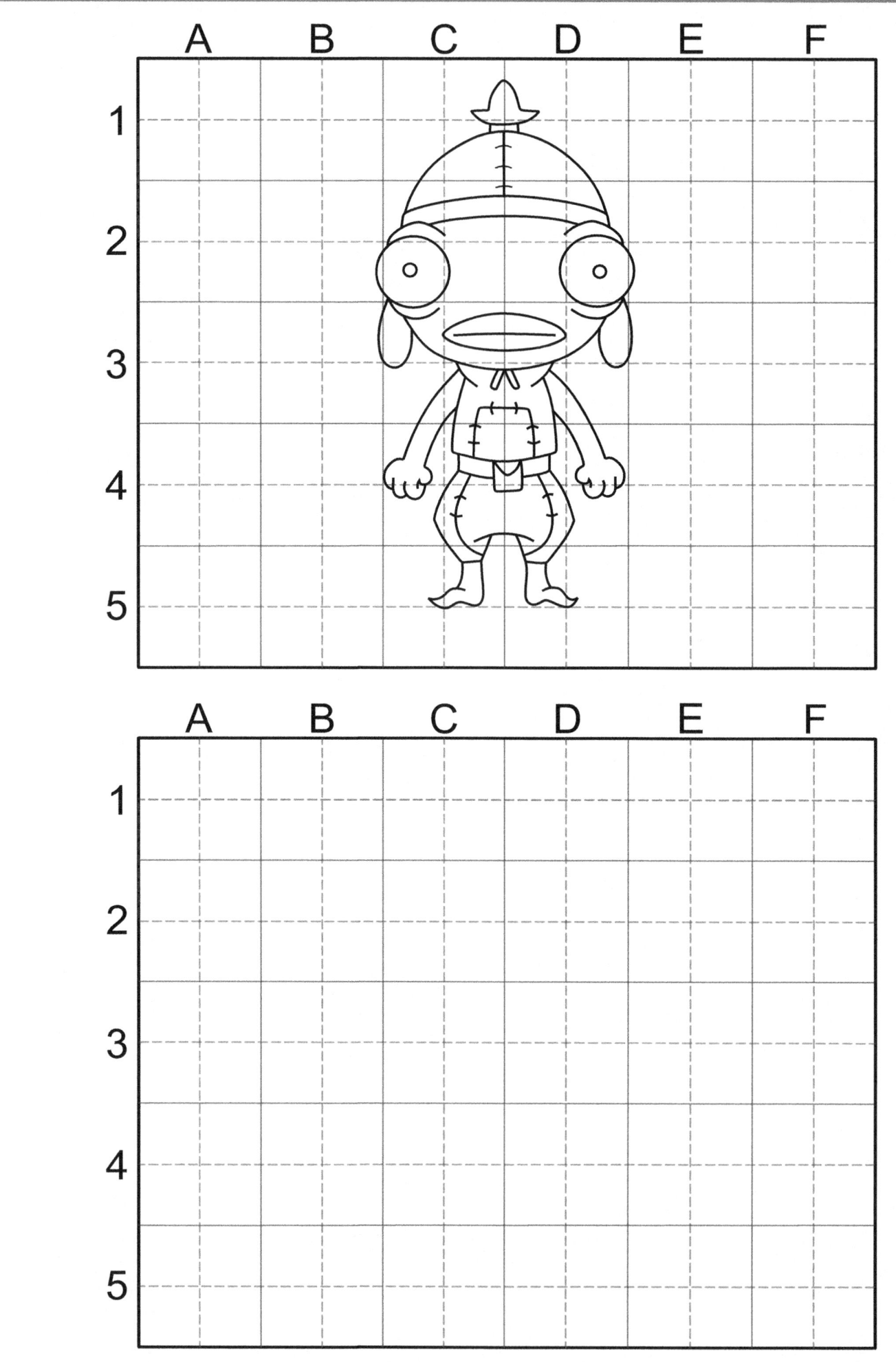

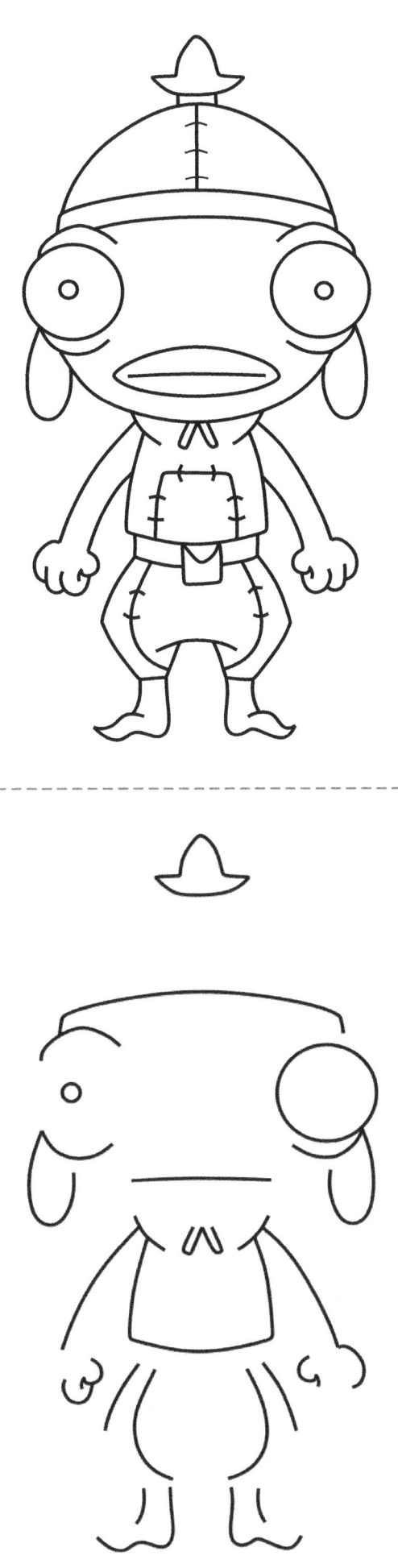

# Your turn !

### Friends ratings

Name : ———— /10   ☆☆☆☆☆   Name : ———— /10

Name : ———— /10              Name : ———— /10

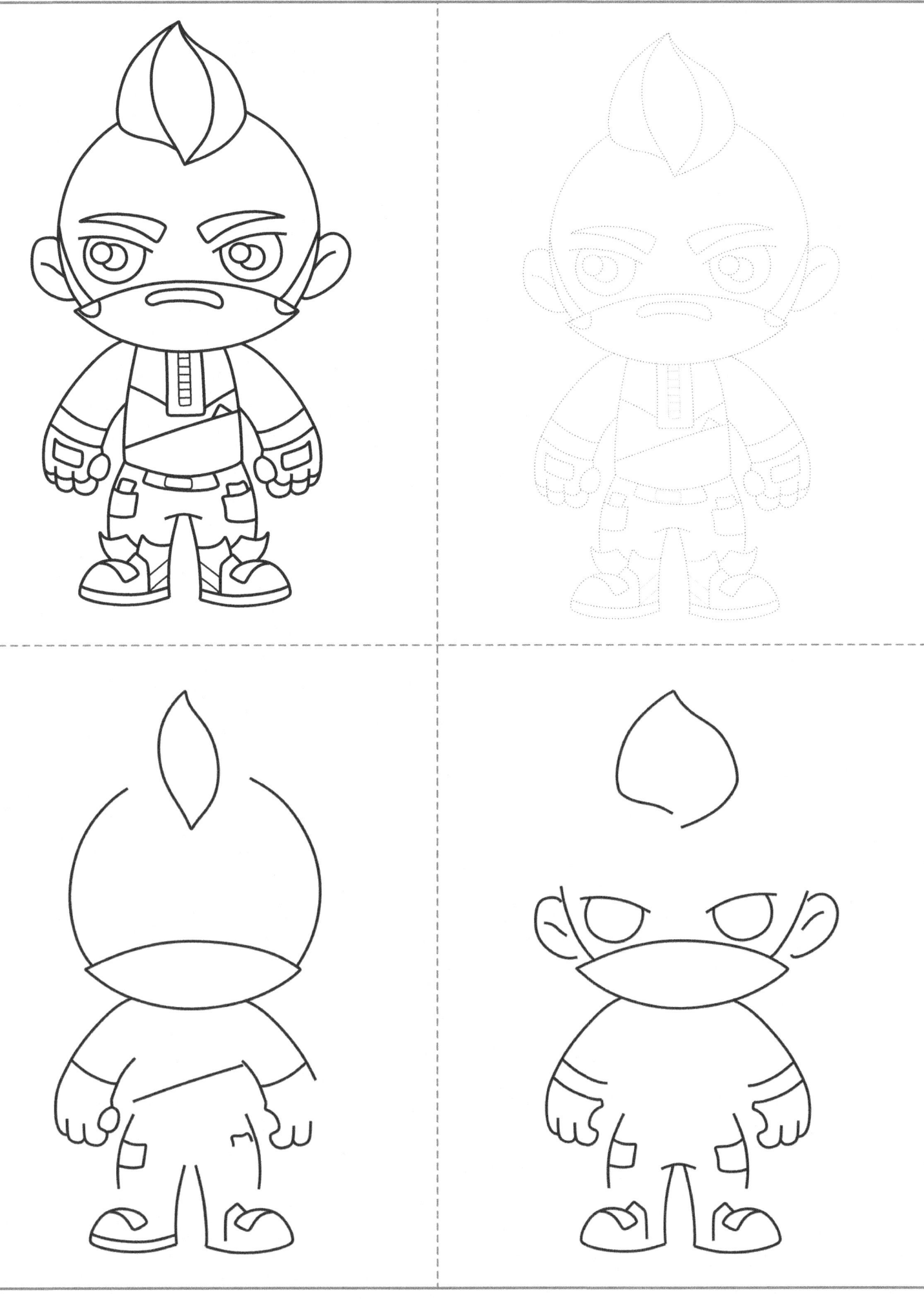

# Your turn !

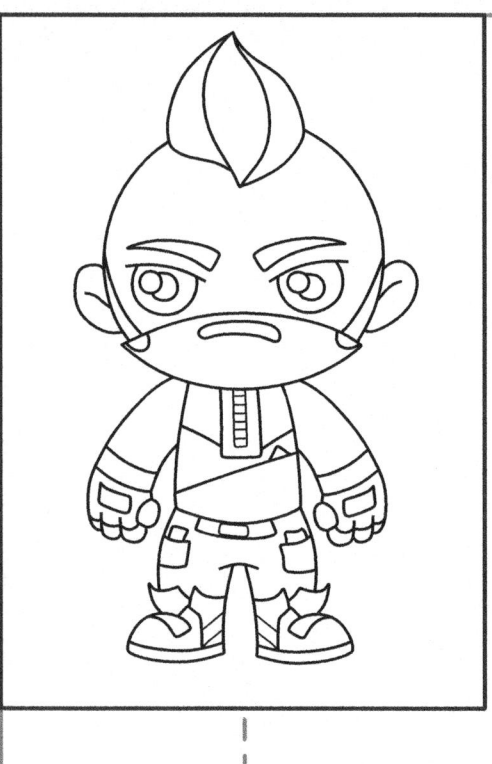

## Friends ratings

Name : ........................ [ /10]      Name : ........................ [ /10]

☆☆☆☆☆

Name : ........................ [ /10]      Name : ........................ [ /10]

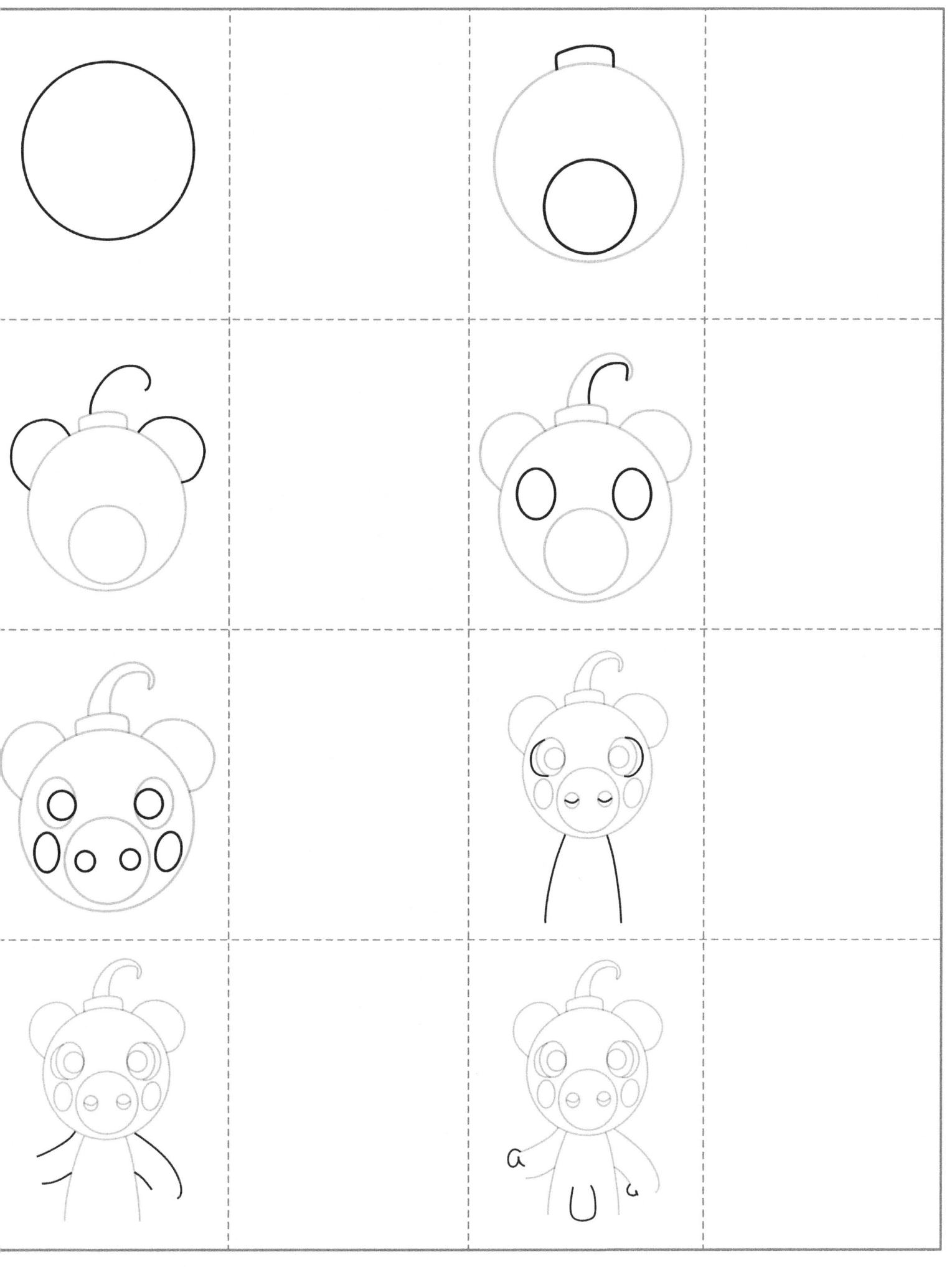

# Your turn !

## Friends ratings

Name : .................... /10

Name : .................... /10

☆ ☆ ☆ ☆ ☆

Name : .................... /10

Name : .................... /10

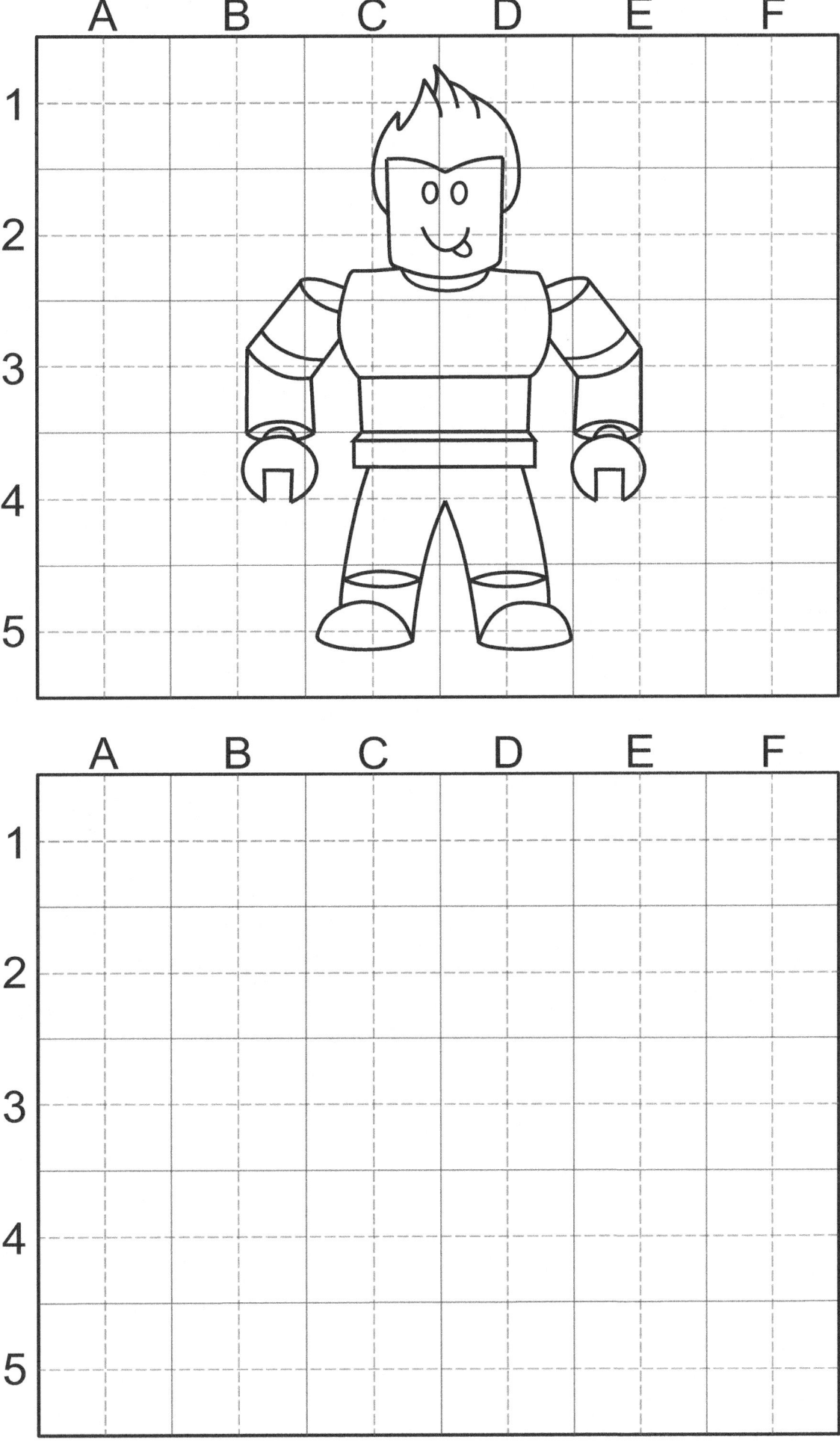

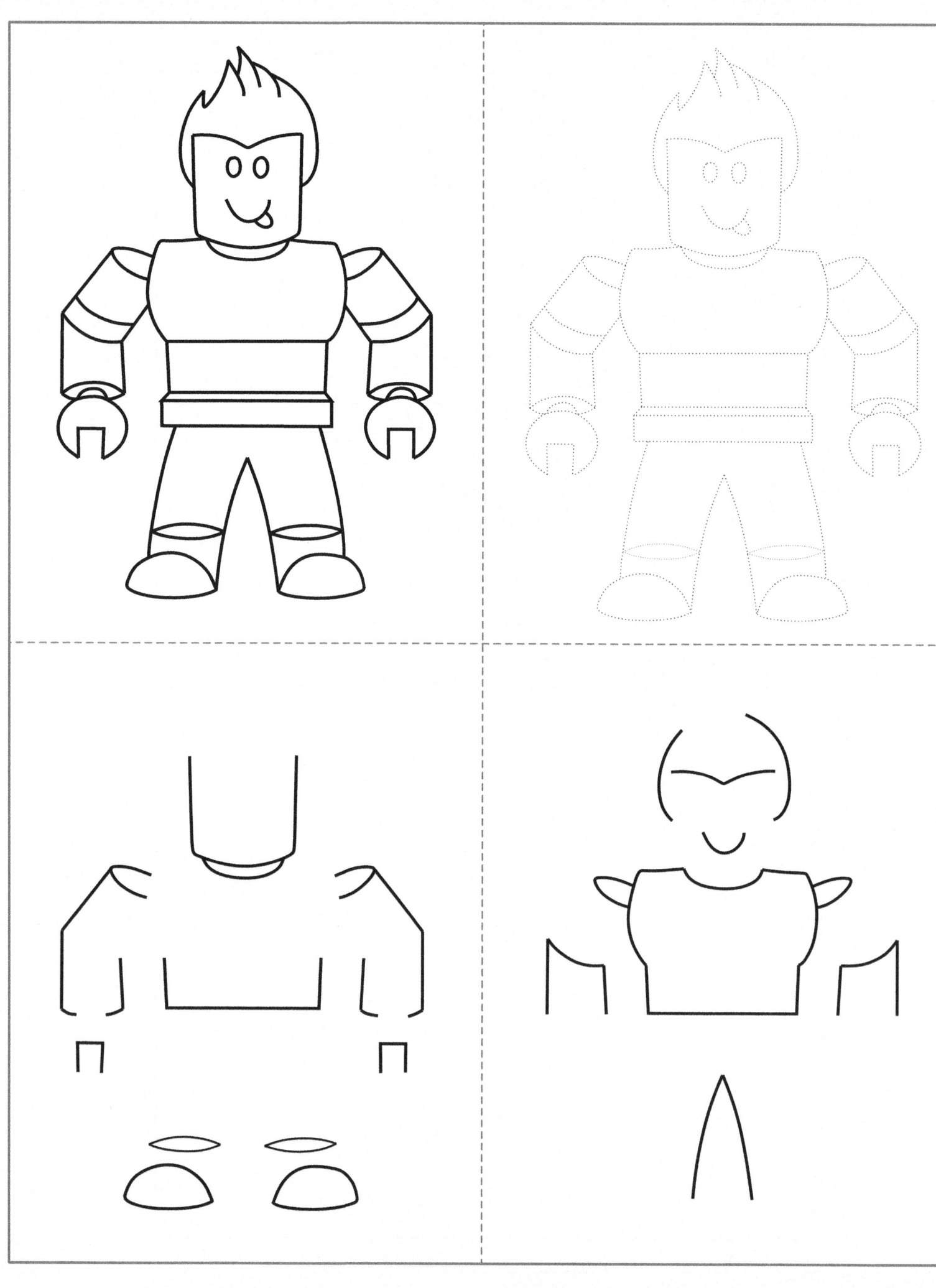

# Your turn !

## Friends ratings

Name : ............... $\overline{10}$

Name : ............... $\overline{10}$

☆☆☆☆☆

Name : ............... $\overline{10}$

Name : ............... $\overline{10}$

# Your turn !

---- Friends ratings ----

Name : _____ $\overline{10}$  ☆☆☆☆☆  Name : _____ $\overline{10}$

Name : _____ $\overline{10}$  Name : _____ $\overline{10}$

# Thank you

## FOR YOUR SUPPORT

Please leave us a review on Amazon
If you are happy with your purchase

We love to hear your opinions/suggestions/comments
to create better products and services for you!
so don't hesitate

All rights are reserved. No part of this publication
may be reproduced, stored in a retrieval system or transmitted
in anyform or by any means, electronic, mechanical, photocopying,
recording or otherwise, without prior permission
of Pro Drawing & Coloring.

Made in the USA
Columbia, SC
06 May 2022